CONTENTS

Radical Force!

The Need for Speed!   6

What Goes Up . . .   8

Gripping Stunts   16

Keeping Your Balance   22

The Force Masters   26

Out of Whack!   28

Glossary   30

Want to Know More?   31

Index   32

Some words are printed in bold, **like this**. You can find out what they mean on page 30. You can also look in the box at the bottom of the page where they first appear.

RADICAL FORCE!

Welcome to the Extreme Zone! This is where a crew of kitesurfers, skateboarders, and skydivers get their thrills. Everyone in the Extreme Zone uses **forces** to get their kicks! Forces are pushes and pulls.

This kitesurfer is in **motion**! She skims across ocean waves at a high speed. She uses a huge kite and the force of the wind. A strong pull can make the kitesurfer fly up into the air. But this can only happen when she hits the right wave!

EXTREME FACT!

The record time for a kitesurf jump is 13.2 seconds in the air!

force	push or pull that makes objects move or change their speed or direction
motion	change of place or position

The Extreme Zone

Chicago, Illinois

Raintree

© 2006 Raintree
Published by Raintree,
an imprint of Capstone Global Library,LLC
Chicago, Illinois

Customer Service   888–454–2279

Visit our website at www.raintreelibrary.com

Printed and bound in China by Leo Paper Group.

12
10 9 8 7 6

Library of Congress Cataloging-in-Publication Data
Mason, Paul, 1967-
  The extreme zone : forces and motion / Paul Mason.
    p. cm.
  Includes bibliographical references and index.
  ISBN 1-4109-1919-6 (library binding) -- ISBN 1-4109-1950-1 (pbk.)
  1. Force and energy--Juvenile literature. 2. Motion--Juvenile
literature. I. Title.
  QC73.4.M387 2004
  531'.6--dc22
                                    2005009538

ISBN 13: 978-1-4109-1950-2

Acknowledgments
The author and publishers are grateful to the following for permission to reproduce copyright material: Action Images p.24–25 (Brandon Malone); Alamy pp.28 b (mediacolors), 28 top (Buzz Pictures), 29 top (Wesley Hitt); Buzz Pictures pp.17 (Leo Sharp), 21 (Ray Wood), 23 (Chris Woodage), 27 (Tim McKenna), 29 b (Neale Haynes); Cadmium p.10 (Imagestate); Digital Vision p.7; Getty Images pp.20, 4–5 (Image Bank), 8–9 (Altrendo); Getty News and Sport p.18–19; Photolibrary.com p.14–15.

Cover photograph of kite skier, reproduced with permission of Getty Images (Photographer's Choice).

Illustrations by Peter Blandamer

The publishers would like to thank Nancy Harris and Harold Pratt for their assistance in the preparation of this book.

Every effort has been made to contact copyright holders of any material reproduced in this book. Any omissions will be rectified in subsequent printings if notice is given to the publishers.

Disclaimer
All the Internet addresses (URLs) given in this book were valid at the time of going to press. However, due to the dynamic nature of the Internet, some addresses may have changed, or sites may have changed or ceased to exist since publication. While the author and publishers regret any inconvenience this may cause readers, no responsibility for any such changes can be accepted by either the author or the publishers.

▼ Kitesurfers use huge kites. Kitesurfers can race along at speeds of over 35 miles (56 kilometers) per hour.

THE NEED FOR SPEED!

Kitesurfers use pulls to make them move. In contrast, skateboarders work with pushes.

Skateboarders can skate along railings. They can do ollies (jumps). They can even flip their board around in the air. Skateboarders need speed to do these tricks. Where do they get their speed? They need to apply a **force**!

A force is a push or pull. Skaters put their boards in **motion** by putting one foot on the ground. They then push down and back with one leg. With each push, their boards pick up more speed. The more skaters push, the faster they can go. Soon, they are going fast enough to do tricks.

Building up speed

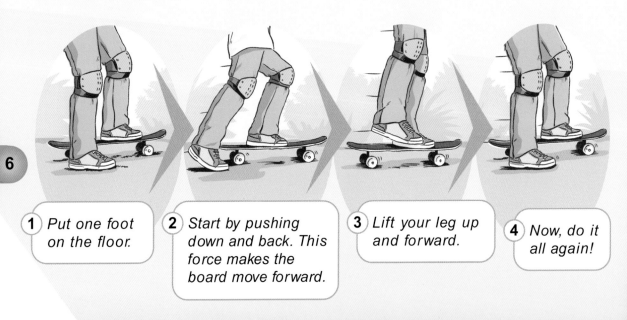

1. *Put one foot on the floor.*
2. *Start by pushing down and back. This force makes the board move forward.*
3. *Lift your leg up and forward.*
4. *Now, do it all again!*

This is a stair jump. ▶
The skater needs a lot
of speed to do this!

7

EXTREME FACT!

The world record for the
highest ollie is 45 inches
(113 centimeters)!

WHAT GOES UP . . .

Most people think jumping out of an airplane is a silly thing to do. Yet skydivers do it for fun!

Skydivers jump from a height of about 15,000 feet (4,600 meters) above the ground. Once skydivers jump, the **force** of **gravity** pulls them down. Gravity is the force that pulls all things toward Earth.

Gravity makes skydivers build up speed as they fall. They **accelerate**. Skydivers can sometimes accelerate to speeds of over 100 miles (160 kilometers) per hour. The best skydivers even do tricks and flips in the air!

accelerate get faster
gravity force that pulls all things toward Earth

GRAVITY PULLS THIS WAY!

◀The skydiver will get faster and faster until he reaches a speed of about 100 miles (160 kilometers) per hour.

EXTREME FACT!

In some competitions, the skydiver tries to land on a target that is just 2 inches (5 centimeters) across!

AIR RESISTANCE

AIR RESISTANCE

The skydiver uses these strings to steer the parachute.

GRAVITY

BRAKING YOUR FALL

A skydiver doesn't want to hit the ground at 100 miles (160 kilometers) per hour! He or she needs to use another **force**, or brake, to slow down.

The skydiver opens a parachute to catch the air. The force of the air hitting the parachute is called **air resistance**. This force pushes against **gravity**. It slows the skydiver down.

You can feel air resistance when riding a bike:

1) You feel more air against you if you ride like this.

2) You feel less air if you crouch down. You can go faster.

air resistance force that slows down an object moving through the air

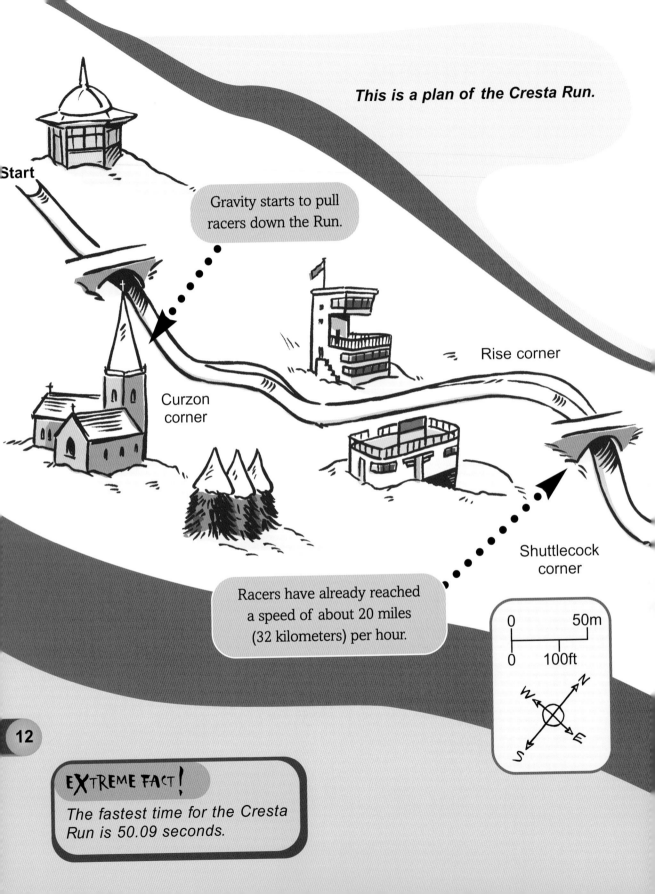

This is a plan of the Cresta Run.

Start

Gravity starts to pull racers down the Run.

Curzon corner

Rise corner

Racers have already reached a speed of about 20 miles (32 kilometers) per hour.

Shuttlecock corner

0 — 50m
0 — 100ft

N
W — E
S

EXTREME FACT!

The fastest time for the Cresta Run is 50.09 seconds.

MAXIMUM SPEED

The Cresta Run is a toboggan course in Switzerland. Every winter, racers come to try their luck at the Run. Like skydivers, these racers love to travel downward quickly. The fastest racers take just over 50 seconds to get down the 4,000-foot (1,212-meter) course!

How do they reach that speed? The course is downhill. The **force** of **gravity** pulls them down. The steeper the hill, the more strongly gravity pulls. This makes the racers go faster. Gravity acts on the racers all the way down the hill. This also makes them **accelerate**, or get faster and faster.

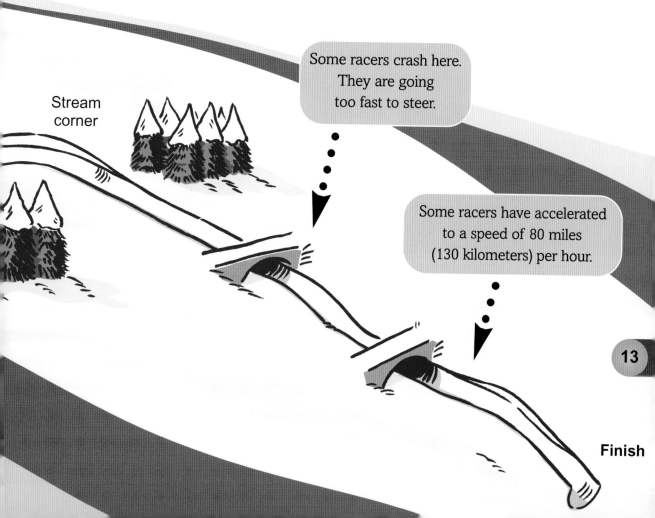

Stream corner

Some racers crash here. They are going too fast to steer.

Some racers have accelerated to a speed of 80 miles (130 kilometers) per hour.

Finish

GETTING AIR

Skydivers and Cresta racers like going down. But most extreme riders want to go up! Snowboarders use **gravity** and a **ramp** to get air. "Get air" means doing a spectacular jump.

First, the snowboarder gets up speed by zooming down a long hill. The **force** of gravity pulls the boarder down, faster and faster.

Then, the boarder hits a type of ramp called a kicker. The ramp turns downward speed into upward **motion**. This causes the boarder to fly into the air!

EXTREME FACT!

The record for the most spins in a snowboard jump is three and a half times!

14

ramp   sloping surface

◄Leaping off a cliff like this takes skill and bravery!

GRAVITY PULLS DOWN

15

Of course the jump doesn't last forever. Gravity is still working, pulling downwards. Now there is only one way to go – down.

GRIPPING STUNTS

This skateboarder is doing a trick called a grind.

Skateboarders can do tricks like this one because the tops of their boards are covered in grip tape. Grip tape is rough like sandpaper. The skateboarder's shoes grip the tape because of a **force** called **friction**. Friction acts when two objects rub against each other.

The skateboarder wants to slide down the rail. For this he needs less friction. The bottom of the board is smooth, and so is the rail. There is little friction between them, so the skateboarder slides quickly.

EXTREME FACT!

The first skateboarders were surfers. Surfers use sticky wax to help their feet grip the board. So the first skateboarders did this too!

friction force that acts between two objects sliding against each other

◄ *This skateboarder also uses **gravity** to help do this trick. Gravity pulls him down the rail.*

This side of the board is rough. The grip tape rubs against the soles of the skater's shoes. There is a lot of friction.

This side of the board is smooth. So is the rail. There is little friction.

PICKS AND BRAKES

Remember the Cresta Run from pages 12–13? Racers on the Run also understand the **force** of **friction**.

Less friction means more speed. Speed is what these racers like! To gain speed they use toboggans with smooth, thin "blades" on the bottom. The blades slide easily over the ice.

Sometimes the racers need friction. They may crash if they go too fast around corners. Cresta racers have "picks" on the toes of their boots. The racers can create friction by dragging the picks on the ice. This makes the toboggan slow down.

EXTREME FACT!

Good, slick ice causes less friction. Racers say "the course is fast" when the ice is slick.

blade

▼ A tobogganist can reach speeds of 80 miles (130 kilometers) per hour. He slows down by using the picks on the toes of his boots.

pick

A FINGERTIP GRIP

Racers on the Cresta Run whizz down as fast as possible. This is the last thing extreme climbers want to do!

The best climbers use only their fingertips and toes to grip the rock. Climbers wear special shoes that have rubber soles. **Friction** between the shoes and the rock stops climbers from slipping.

A climber can press down with either shoe. This creates more friction between the shoe and the rock. This means the climber's foot stays in place.

Most climbers hate rain. Water gets between their shoes and the rock. This means there is less friction. The shoes do not grip as well and the rock becomes slippery. Climbers are much more likely to fall in the rain.

EXTREME FACT!

Some climbs in California's Yosemite Valley are so long they take days to finish!

▼ If climbers slip, **gravity** takes over. They fall down. The safety rope stops them before they hit the ground.

rubber sole

KEEPING YOUR BALANCE

Extreme athletes often use **forces** to move. But sometimes the goal is to stay still. The trick in this photo might look easy. However, standing a bike on its front wheel is very hard.

Knowing about **balanced forces** helps extreme riders. All the forces acting on this rider are in balance. The rider doesn't move.

In this trick, **gravity** is pulling down on the rider and the bike. The ground is pushing up on the bike's wheel. The biker holds the back of the bike. He uses his muscles to balance his weight. Gravity will make him fall if he leans the wrong way. All the forces are equal, or in balance, and so the rider doesn't move.

EXTREME FACT!

The best-known freestyle BMX rider is Dave Mirra. He has won the World Championship ten times!

balanced forces   when forces have equal strength and work in opposite directions

It takes a lot of ▶
balance to hold
a bike like this!

GRAVITY PULLS DOWN

GROUND PUSHES UP

23

RIDING AT SPEED

This cyclist doesn't want to stay still. He wants to win his race! **Balanced Forces** help him.

Balanced forces can make something stay still. But forces are also balanced if something is moving at a speed that stays the same.

This rider is moving at 40 kilometres (25 miles) per hour. His speed isn't changing. This is because the forces on him are in balance.

At least one of the forces ▶ will have to change if this rider wants to go faster. For example, he could pedal harder.

PEDAL POWER

constant   staying the same

Three main forces affect the cyclist:

- The rider's pedaling pushes the bike forwards
- **Friction** acts between the tires and the ground
- **Air resistance** pushes against the bike and rider.

The rider will keep going at the same speed if all of these forces stay **constant**.

AIR RESISTANCE

FRICTION ON TIRES

THE FORCE MASTERS

Imagine how powerful all the water in this photo must be. Why isn't the surfer crushed by it? Because she's a **force** master!

The wave rushes toward the beach. The surfer turns her board so that it catches the force of the wave. The surfer is pushed along the wave away from the crashing water.

There are plenty of force masters in extreme sports. Skateboarders and climbers are rulers of **friction**. Friction is the force that keeps them from falling. Snowboarders and skydivers play with **gravity**. Gravity is the force that keeps them moving.

You can be a force master, too. Get out there and do it! You don't need someone to force you!

▼ *This surfer is "tubed" inside the wave. This is the ultimate move in surfing!*

OUT OF WHACK!

Even **force** masters sometimes make mistakes when they try to control forces!

This rider was trying to keep ▶ all the forces in balance so that he wouldn't move. But a force changed. He lost his balance!

▼ ***Gravity** has **accelerated** this rider down the hill. Now, he is going too fast. It looks like he is out of control!*

This climber needed ▶
friction to keep her grip.
Without enough friction,
she has slid off the rock!

◀ Gravity is about to
pull this surfer down
into the wave. Surfers
sometimes call waves
"the washing machine."
This surfer is about to
go in the spin cycle!

GLOSSARY

accelerate get faster. A cyclist accelerates by pedaling more quickly.

air resistance force that slows down an object moving through the air. Bigger objects meet more air resistance than smaller objects.

balanced forces when forces have equal strength and work in opposite directions. Balanced forces make an object stay still or move at a constant speed.

constant staying the same. A cyclist's speed stays constant if it does not change.

force push or pull that makes objects move or change their speed or direction. The force of the wind pulls a kitesurfer along at a high speed.

friction force that acts between two objects sliding against each other. Friction helps your feet grip a skateboard.

gravity force that pulls all things toward Earth. Gravity pulls skydivers toward the Earth when they jump out of airplanes.

motion change of place or position. A car is in motion if it is moving.

ramp sloping surface. A ramp can be used by a snowboarder to "get air."

WANT TO KNOW MORE?

There's a lot to know about extreme sports! These are some other books to read:

BOOKS

- Cooper, Christopher. *Forces and Motion: From Push to Shove*. Chicago: Heinemann Library, 2004.

- Dick, Scott. *BMX*. Chicago: Heinemann Library, 2002.

- Farndon, John. *Gravity, Weight and Balance*. Tarrytown, N.Y.: Marshall Cavendish, 2002.

- Fullick, Ann. *Under Pressure: Forces*. Chicago: Heinemann Library, 2005.

- Gikow, Louise. *Extreme Sports: A Chapter Book*. Danbury: Scholastic, 2004.

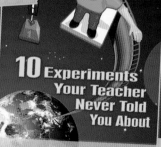

Knowing about forces also comes in handy when you're attacking a castle. To find out why, read ***Castle Under Siege!***

You may not think so, but it is possible to escape gravity. To find out how, try reading ***10 Experiments Your Teacher Never Told You About***.

INDEX

acceleration 8, 13, 28

air resistance 11, 25

balanced forces 22–23, 24, 28

bikers 22–23, 28

climbers 20–21, 26, 29

control, loss of 28–29

Cresta Run 12–13, 18, 20

cyclists 11, 24–25

forces 4, 6, 8, 11, 13, 14, 16, 18, 22, 24–25

friction 16, 17, 18, 20, 25, 26, 29

getting air 14

gravity 8, 11, 12, 13, 14, 15, 17, 21, 22, 26, 28, 29

grip tape 16, 17

jumps 6, 7, 14, 15

kitesurfers 4–5, 6

motion 4, 6, 14

ollies 6, 7

parachutes 10, 11

pulls 4, 6, 8, 13, 14, 15, 17, 22

pushes 6, 22, 25

ramps 14

skateboarders 6–7, 16–17, 26

skydivers 8–11, 26

slowing down 11, 18, 19

snowboarders 14–15, 26, 28

speed 5, 6, 8, 9, 12, 13, 14, 18, 19, 24

surfers 16, 26–27, 29

tobogganists 12–13, 18–19

world records 4, 7, 12, 14